LETTERS TO MY HAPPY PLACE

SHRITESH KUSHWAHA

This book is dedicated to someone whose name I can't take, so it's dedicated in peace

for my love

Contents

Acknowledgements   *vii*

Prologue   *ix*

  1. Story Of A Heartbreak   1

  2. I Hate Love Stories   4

  3. Her Silence   5

  4. My Only Wish   7

  5. Words Of Promise   9

  6. My Experiences Of Love   11

  7. Possibilities   13

  8. My Daydream   14

  9. The Secrets I Hold   15

10. My Missing Something   17

11. When Roads Diverge   19

12. I Chose You   21

13. It Isn't Heartbreak   23

14. A Tiny Hope   25

15. My Constant   27

16. After You   29

17. Why I Write?   30

18. The Stranger   32

19. An Ordinary Man   34

20. I Want Somethings   36

21. The Lies Of Eyes   37

22. I Had A Dream   38

23. Endings And Goodbyes   39

24. A Rebel Or A Traveler   40

25. A Naive To Think Free   41

26. A Mute   42

Contents

27. Regret   43

28. Nothing To Me   44

29. The Fear I Feared   45

30. A Gone Voice   46

31. My Peace   47

32. My Almost Story   48

33. A Hoax Called Freedom   50

34. A Grave Marked Unknown   51

35. A Restart I Would Like   52

36. Distance From The World   53

37. A Good Change   54

38. A Shattered Heart   55

39. A Failure   57

40. September   59

41. It's You   60

42. My Burning Ship   61

43. The Unwritten Poem   63

Acknowledgements

This collection of poems is my work of past year or so, and I'm very grateful to each and every person who read these poems. I would also like to thank my teachers for making me aware of my love for literature also I would like to thank my friends who read my early drafts and gave me appreciation for writing, without you all this book would never have existed.

Lastly, I would again like to thank all my readers. I hope this book gives you the sense of love, awe. Travel and issues with which I have written. And remember , this book is as much as yours as it is mine.

Love

Shritesh

Prologue

A teenage boy fell in Love with someone he would have never thought, altering his conciousness for life, making him believe in love and fall in it. But also as time passes he believes in fate, if it's not meant to happen it won't happen making him uniterested in things for life, a heartbroken for life.

1. Story of a Heartbreak

My world came crashing down,
As, the name echoed in my ears,
Unlocking the greatest fear,
The fear, what if?
She's not into me?
I'm not the one?
will I be the forgotten one?
Will she remember me?
How will I be I ?
All the fear came,
Took him to oblivion,
Shook him to the core,
What was all it for?
I asked,
With tears rolling down the eyes,
For a moment he thought,
That What has fate brought,
He wanted to tell her everything,
His emotions and feeling,
He whispered,
I really liked you, you know,
He stuttered,
As his eyes blurred,
He turned away from her,
Hiding his tears,
Thinking what has fate brought again,
One of the fears to trade again,

Inside, He was dead again….
Courageously he put up the facade again,
That he's not dead,
Broken smile on his face,
Hiding his pain with no trace,
Her hand on the shoulder,
Felt like wonder,
Thinking who was to blame,
Afterall she wasn't his's to claim,
Broken as one can be,
He decided to walk again,
Putting up a facade for the pain,
Didn't knew if she understood,
Or for her, he's just pile of woods,
To burn,
Doubted his steps on every turn,
Was he wrong to,
let things take the natural course,
He asked feeling's source,
He asked and asked his heart,
Why? Why?
Why him always?
Why can't be be,
happy for once?
Loved for once?
Why it always has to be him?
Why this time, when,
He thought someone would chose him first,
The end of his love thirst,
All he wanted to be loved,
Truly loved,

for once, loved.......

2. I hate love stories

Well she asked,

why do I hate love stories,

I said-:

It's not the stories I hate,

It's the endings of fate ,

That I hate,

THE HAPPILY EVER AFTER ,

does it ever happens in life,

Sure doesn't in mine,

What was my crime?

I asked,

And asked again and again,

But all in vain,

Adding to the agony and pain,

There comes the clouds,

The bearer of lover's shrouds,

Upon him, showering their sorrow,

Like there's no tomorrow,

In the rain,

Thinking of his tries,

He cries and cries.....

3. Her silence

Wind whistling down her ears,
Her eyes sparkling with tears of fear,
Her glasses making the path blurry,
With her heart filled with fury,
She was walking with her hopes up,
With a friend to cheer her up,
Walking down the deserted road,
The two were talking of,
Their fears , of their insecurities,
The hopes and the worries,
Cut-off from both their worlds,
Far from the crowd,
At-par with staying and leaving,
They were talking of,
The life's dilemma,
Putting everything at coma,
Looking at the stars above ,
Blue sky and the road ahead,
They thought to wait,
Sitting on the bench,
Uttering no word to other,
Yet understanding the other,
The lamp flickering in the shades of winter,
Words spoken were like splinters,
Silence was all they needed,
There was silence,
A heartening silence,

Shutting down the violence of,
Fears and tears,
There was hope again,
The fears were gone,
Tears soon,
Glasses as clear as crystal,
She, as steady as centennial,
The was she,
With her heads up and hopes again,
Ready to conquer the world,
Once again......

4. My only wish

What do I want?
What do I wish?
Who is she to you?
She's the wish I had,
A wish, that I wanted her,
A wish to hug her,
And never let go,
To hold hands while we walk,
To gaze into those deep brown eyes,
and make her mine,
She's the wish I had,
All it ever will be ,
The wish I had,
A wish,
A wish to call you home,
A wish to say your name,
A wish to grow old together,
To hold your heart forever,
Every time I see you,
I remember,
You were the wish I had
I wish,
I was the book you read,
The fragrance you wear,
The voices you hear,
To be the Light in your life,
You to be,

forever my wife,

I wish,

You weren't the wish I had,

I wish you were by my side,

Every time I wake up,

You were the wish I had,

Maybe you were not perfect,

But you're the wish I wished for.....

5. Words of Promise

A meak, pale voice ,
clouded his ears,
he turned to see the tears,
like pearls settling in her eyes,
uncontrollable,
despite the tries,
not word, not kerchief
he had nothing to give her,
to stop the pearls settling,
but,
kept trying,
reminding her of her,
constant clearing of her eyes,
as her tears drained her heart,
nonchalant about the world around,
heart's tale was about to start,
with her guard down,
her voice making her mind's face,
the eyes,
making the heart's case,
as the,
tissue soaked in the tears,
the night of the fears,
disappears,
as the sleeves became wet,
motion of the leaves was set,
a little sound of music,

making life less chaotic,
with her eyes dried,
the clouds cried,
tear me,
with your fears,
your tears,
said the tissue,
and as his bits and pieces were made,
the tears fade,
and ,
the promises were made......

6. My experiences of love

I don't know , what were you wearing,
but I sure did knew, what my heart was hearing,
and how it got beating,
besting all my senses,
And to top it all of,
the way you glanced at me,
If you could read my eyes,
you would have read everything,
If you had seen my face,
you would have known everything,
If you would have said YES ,
you would have been everything......
Sometimes I do wonder ,
May be I wasn't ready,
May be you were the one,
Or may be you were not,
But now that,
You are gone,
May be I'm ready to accept,
May be I'm not,
And it keeps getting harder,
May be I want it this way,
May be I don't ,
May be I want to talk it away,
or May be walk it away,
May be I don't,
or May be I won't....

May be I'm too afraid now,
afraid, of love?
Or falling in love,
Or of one sided love,
or not falling in love,
or falling in love harder?
I guess, I don't know....
that am I afraid of, about love?
Maybe of my experience, with love,
love for me, is,
The love for the eternity,
which I will neither get nor I will be able to forget,
the love for me now,
Is the matter to be not tangled with,
just let it be as it is, cause it's love,
the chief of mischieves,
culprit of all the stories,
the pain in all the memories,
the wishes in all our dairies,
it's love,
love.......

7. Possibilities

As I looked down,
At my feet ,
There it was,
Bits and pieces....
Holding, hiding,
The moments I hardly met,
Soaked with the comets,
Lying there.....
Like a night full of stars,
Concealing Darkness of the scars,
Lying there....
Swallowing, Burying,
meteors,
Of fallen hope,
Of broken scope,
Sheeted by,
the shredded cloak,
Lying there....
Lying there,
It Carries within,
The diversity of the duality,
The possibility and the reality,
Of What happened,
And ,
what never will happen....

8. My Daydream

All the eyes in the world,
And yet,
Here I am,
Always finding yours....
And today, You saw,
Me,
Admiring, Adoring you,
I felt like getting caught,
Red handed,
Red faced,
As your eyes glared,
In your own, sarcastic way,
As your eyes rolled,
I rolled with them,
causing all sorts of mayhem,
in my heart, my brain.......
And as I was,
cherishing the moments,
you,
you blinked,
and my dream,
remains a dream........

9. The secrets I hold

Every time,

I see you,

I have half a mind to,

Walk right past you,

Or be the bystander as you pass.....

Cause I'm afraid,

Afraid as,

I still get the butterflies,

They talk about,

You,

The secret I don't talk about.....

Afraid of my eyes,

That they'll spill the truth,

And yet Every time I fail,

And still dare,

To stay,

In the midst of all reasons,

Always look for the one to stay,

All the reasons to walk,

And I find the only one to talk...

And Every time when you say ,BYE,

I feel betrayed,

Betrayed by life, by happiness,

By the cosmos,

As if it conspired,

to give everything but YOU......

And if I ever meet you again,

I wish,

it's the way we did,

I love you all over again,

I would prefer the life which includes you,

than the one, that doesn't,

Even if I have to suffer,

You are the life that I'd prefer.....

And ,

If I never meet you again,

My memories of us, is,

A storm,

Bearing a rose,

That rose in my heart's sea,

And turbulates the silent sea,

Every time.......

10. My missing something

I feel something empty,
I'm missing something....
I miss you,
I miss talking with you,
sitting on that bench,
gossiping with you,
taking turns,
on most ridiculous questions,
with utmost sincerity, and
talking with pure genuity,
noting, nothing there,
just us,
sitting on the bench, by the garden.....
I'm missing,
the best part of my day,
you,
even I didn't realize that,
but you were, the best part,
i wasn't sure, you were her,
but now I'm,
And,
now you are gone,
just like that,
gone.....
I don't know how many compliments,
gifts and letters,
I have for you,

but I can't dare give you,
it's not that,
I don't want to give you,
with all my heart, I Want,
but i just can't.....
I can't even tell you,
I miss you,
I can't tell,
how deep did I fell for you,
I can't tell you,
that,
I miss my heart,
I miss you,,
with all my heart.....

11. When roads diverge

What happens,
When the roads diverge,
The addresses change,
The dresses soon.....
Unspoken are the words,
Unsent are the letters,
Withholding the stories,
Of sins and the nobility,
Of greed and the prosperity,
The love and the hate,
What happens?
when the roads diverge....
When the roads diverge,
The co-passengers change,
the passerby's too,
the vehicles change,
but the traveller remains,
when the paths diverge,
lost are the emotions that emerged.....
What happens,
When the roads diverge,
the faces become memories,
convos become diaries,
convoys become parties,
waiting becomes eternity,
time becomes, the greatest frailty.....
When the roads diverge,

and the raids on present, are done,
I have met everyone, but,
the one, So,
the road will diverge again,
just to converge again.....

12. I chose you

I chose you,
I chose to love you,
despite the difficulties,
and the negative possibilities,
I chose you,
despite our differences
and the distances,
I chose to love....
I chose,
the sufferings of love,
the wonders
and the thunders of it,
for you,
I chose love,
even if,
you didn't care, but,
I wasn't the one to spare,
and,
I chose to love,
all the time in the world,
and I chose to spend it, waiting,
waiting for something to happen,
that I knew would never happen,
knowing well, it's not fate,
but the choice I made,
to love you.....
even if,

this is, the last of us,
and,
You and I will never be us,
I still choose to love,
to love you,
like the meeting of,
the night and day,
like the meetings,
on the horizon,
like the love of stars,
I chose to love you,
to love you from a far......

13. It isn't Heartbreak

It isn't heartbreak,
is it?
if we never dated,
then, being separated,
isn't heartbreak, is it?
then the increased distances,
and the changed stances,
even if,
we knew each other,
you didn't bother,
to talk,
you just walked,
then it isn't heartbreak, is it?
our shared stories,
all those climbed stories,
count for nothing?
do they???
heartbreak or not,
we didn't tie the knot....
stances changed for a reason,
distance was not the reason for sure,
and my intention was all pure,
to not talk,
and just walk,
walking did hurt us, but,
talking would have broken us,
or just me,

or, I didn't have it in me,

to walk after the talk,

so I chose to walk......

Now,

I don't know,

if we were meant to be or not,

or we were just,

too good to be true,

but I know,that,

if we never dated,

cause we always waited,

for the other to bother .....

I guess,

I don't know,

whether it's heartbreak,

or it isn't?

maybe it's something,

or maybe it isn't,

maybe there's nothing to comprehend,

or,

maybe be it is the end..........................

14. A tiny hope

Driving down the slope,

with a glimmer of hope,

having locked the steering,

and failed brakes,

embracing all the mistakes,

realizing the way it is,

no shortcuts or an underpass,

or any way to just surpass.....

but what it's for?

i wonder,

as my thoughts start to ponder,

what does one need,

what is that, one wants?

i don't know that,

but, I,

I need you,

I want to be yours,

In this life,

in the next and the next after that.....

Just YOU and I,

figuring out everything,

walking on nothing,

riding on the road,

at each other side,

sitting on the beach,

and watch every tide,

YOU and I...

In the face of complete darkness,
with no more thoughts to harness,
My thoughts started binding,
and I, realizing,
realizing what I have,
and who I don't,
your presence that i have,
and the essence that, I don't
the heartless body, I have,
and the heart, I don't......

15. My constant

In the world full of big moments,
and enormous promises
and grand gestures,
I'll be the little joys,
you meet everyday,
like the sun glancing across the window,
like the moon looking down the willow,
the sunset clouds of the evening,
chirping birds of the morning,
or the little moments you cherish,
the little gestures you wish,
I'll be,
the smile,
of the insignificant gift received,
of the good deeds perceived,
the smile,
of meeting the favorite ,
of watching the favorite show....
I'll be,
the smile of the favorite dress,
a life with no stress ,
take all your pains,
with no distress....
In a world full of dark alleys,
you are my light,
the light that gives me my sight,
In a world where,

change is the only constant,

you are the constant, that doesn't change........

16. After you

After You
After you,
is what I have always said,
you, for forever, are my always,
though I never wanted,
but that's how it fell,
a story to tell.....
After you,
is what I'll always say,
whenever someone asks,
asks of my poems and the lines,
the subject and it's fines,
you and after you,
is what I'll them,
over a glass of wine.....
whenever they ask,
ask will i forever live like me?
whether I want to ,
or I need to live
my life,
with you not in it,
but i have to,
is what I tell them,
after you......

17. Why I write?

I write,
I write things,
that i can't suppress
so I Write, to express,
express my heart,
its fires and desires,
it's should be's and may be's......
I write ,
I write to feel alive,
to speak my mind,
to speak of my day,
I write,
to lay some baggage on the way.....
I Write,
and i tell stories,
to diaries,
as they listen,
and speak to none,
and keep for, the one......
I write,
I write dreams,
dreams that never came,
disappointment the reality became.....
You know,
I write,
I write cause I'm afraid,
afraid to tell you,

afraid of you leaving,
so never tell,
that,
I write you.........

18. The stranger

Drinking,
in a tavern,
I see a lantern,
burning in a cottage,
of great Lineage....
I see a stranger,
a stranger,
i pursued towards,
for light,
to evade the night,
to reach for wisdom,
to build a king's Kingdom....
now the light flickers,
and the night whispers,
Whispers, it's charms,
the charms of silence,
born of violence,
violence,
of the dimming brightness,
and the glowing darkness.....
the flickering light flashes,
flashes guilt,
and the regrets that built,
regrets that I have now,
regrets in different aspects,
regrets of different prospects,
regrets of all sort....

regret that,

you are the stranger,

I met,

that i never meant to,

to be a stranger again,

you are the stranger,

that i wanted to be mine,

mine for the lifetime,

for every lifetime........

19. An ordinary man

The night whispers,

And the shadows listen,

The moon shines,

And the grave glows,

A bouquet wearied,

On that,

Grave marked unknown,

I rest,

After the battle,

And the violence,

there remained,

the silence,

The silence of eternity,

An ordinary man,

In a special world,

Resting in my grave....

Maybe it takes something,

Something special,

To be a radical,

To be complete,

And

I'm just an ordinary man,

In special person's world,

Resting in my grave....

And if I'm to be born again,

I'll want to be a bird,

A bird of it's will,

To soar above everything,
Fly across everything,
To surrender to no cage,
To no bondage of age...
A bird , I wish,
As an ordinary man,
In a special person's world......

20. I want somethings

Well, they said-:
You are perfect,
what could you be wanting,
you smile, tells you lost nothing,
and your calmness,
well it tells you have everything.....
I replied:-
no one's perfect,
my smile, it's a broken one,
the one, you never want,
and
there are things that i want,
sometimes,
i want,
to release the withholded storm,
to shower all the voices upon,
to shut up the voices in my head,
to have a peaceful sleep in my bed,
to make tears stop before the oceans dry,
to dissipate the myth that I don't cry,
there i things i want,
sometimes.......

21. The lies of eyes

The eyes,
They never lie,
So they say,
But I wonder,
Does mine ever speaks?
Or your's ever believe?
And so,
We both grieve,
With our glowy red eyes,
Oceans deep memories,
That define our stories,
Of,
the past that didn't last,
The future that didn't nurture,
And ,
In the presence of present,
With our story cresent,
We grieve and believe,
Eyes never lie.....

22. I had a dream

Dream,
I once had it,
a will to fight to reach it,
to conquer the road that came along,
to live the fame,
I once had a dream,
And it had a name
It wasn't real ,
and yet it felt,
I was a dreamer,
And so I knelt,
to the dream with a name
I had the relief,
as the dream brought relief,
belief in me, my destiny,
and,
why flow with the stream?
why not dream?
I once had a dream,
and it had a name....

23. Endings and Goodbyes

The endings, the goodbyes,
what are they worth,
Do they mean sometime more,
or just another wave on the shore,
or is it just the acceptance,
of my penance,
that I enjoy the sunset,
even if the night comes later......
But YOU,
mean something more,
divine to the core,
oh I wonder,
what is this something could mean?
the ending of what could have been......
On the shore of endings, goodbyes
where they fear to tread,
I stand here on the edge,
thinking,
is this the goodbye for forever,
to not say a word,
to my heart's endeavour........

24. A rebel or A traveler

• 40 •

The art of artistry,

to conjure the mystery,

to make desire,

from the rues of sapphire,

to be a wanderer,

not the rebel but the traveller.....

To soar the canvas,

the sunset paints,

to pour the delight,

when the night faints,

to belong to the skies,

to be the one who flies.....

A life of imperfections,

of raw expressions,unheard impression,

A life for the heart,

in the nature's art,

A life of nothing, but,

but a mere wonder,

a life of an explorer,

not the rebel but the traveler.......

25. A naive to think free

On a bridge,

watching drops brush the trees,

sound of rain that frees,

devours melancholy,

all the unholy,

the darkness of eternity,

brings some serenity,

to not have wishes,

but stories,

to be a vessel of memories,

on that rugged shelf of life,

to be the journal with stories,

in a dreamy sky of paradise,

to go beyond fright,

flight of my own kite,

to sail in the winds' car,

to flow with the water afar,

in a boat, so carefree,

to be a soul so naive,

Naive to think, and be free,

to be a raindrop on a tree,

free to flow and rest,

to exist of my own zest....

26. A mute

I can write a hundred letters,
just not the words I want to say,
I can know a hundred languages,
a hundred dialects,
but,
I can never who you are to me, or
what you mean to me.....

27. Regret

I want to punch something,
something so hard,
that it shatters my hand,
shatters the thought to write you,
the thought of belongingness,
that you belong with me,
and it still shatters my heart,
that your's isn't mine.....

28. Nothing to me

you are nothing to me,
and yet,
i close my eyes,
and i see a face,
a face so serene,
of charms as serene....
A face that's nothing
the nothing from a scenery,
the nothing etched on clouds,
the nothing that made my shroud,
the nothing which means something......
A nothing to go up and beyond,
a nothing that has my peace,
A nothing to be wished,
A nothing to be cherished,
a nothing to die for,
and yet it's nothing.....
I close my eyes,
and I forget,
forget that,
You are nothing to me,
and I'm nothing to you.....

29. The fear I feared

• 45 •

The fear I feared,
has begotten,
the song that I wrote,
is long forgotten.....
Thoughts,
of my dark corner,
ventured upon a hill,
song of a stranger,
killed in time's mill....
A song once promised,
for love,
is now buried,
with its tunes and love,
in the dunes......
The song of a story,
of once rich glory,
is now,
just a memory,
of some mnemonics,
of once good lyrics....
The song that I wrote,
was once besotten,
but now,
it's long forgotten.......

30. A gone voice

From the echoes of silence,
I heard a voice,
a voice with a tone,
A tone I knew to have gone...
A sound that I hallucinate,
A sound that echoes in closed walls,
A sound that I wait for,
A sound that I like a little more,
the illusion I love a little longer ......
But,
is the waiting right?
why am I waiting,
for the chapter to get over?
or for the chamber to be empty?
of the voice that echoes....
Of my dark quiet soul,
the voice heard my silence,
the voice with a tone,
A tone I knew to have gone......

31. My peace

Peace,

I had my peace,

and then it was taken,

by a gaze of eyes,

a thousand thoughts,

a million voices in my head,

all at once took my peace,

and teased me, for forever......

I remember,

I wrote a letter,

for the letter,

that was never written,

with words,

that were. never spoken.....

Sometimes, I wonder,

is it really fate,

or a game of chance,

a flip of a coin,

to determine,

why someone would never be mine?

But now, I have peace,

as in,

the beauty of broken things,

the flight of severed wings,

but deep down I remember,

It's a game of chance,

and I lost mine.....

32. My almost story

Within these four walls,
Of my room,
Buried are my secrets,
Of my oceanic eyes,
The mirror upon these Walls,
Knows all my stories,
Even the story of ALMOST,
how I was almost happy....
These walls know,
the conversation I almost made,
How I wasn't interested,
In love,
Then I almost had you,
As if written by the creator,
But now,
I'm almost a stranger.....
The finished cigarettes,
With echoes of all my regrets,
How I almost succeeded,
In forgetting a name,
A name that was,s
Almost mine,
A story that was,
Almost made,
How I was,
Almost in love,
How I was,

Almost good enough......

33. A hoax called freedom

Freedom,
An idea that I'm free,
Free of my will,
Free of my choices,
Is all a hoax….
I'm free to find the enemy,
And it's everywhere,
In the alley here,
On the sidewalk there,
I see my enemy,
In the monsters live,
The reapers of my life,
I'm free to see,
My dreams burning,
Desires flaming ,
To see my body scorched,
To feel my soul dead…
I'm free ,
To be burned in fire,
No woods, but of my ire,
My soul to be captured,
In this very place,
To get everything but solace,
I'm free,
Of this monster's kingdom
Free of a hoax freedom….

34. A grave marked unknown

Things untold,
are starting to unfold,
as my vision grows darker,
and lie reveals itself,
truth hits harder,
and now i rest,
on a Grave marked unknown.....
The night whispers,
And the shadows listen,
The moon shines,
And the grave glows,
A bouquet wearied,
On that,
Grave marked unknown,
I rest,
After the battle,
And the violence,
there remains,
a silence,
a silence for eternity,
for an ordinary man,
who pretended to be brave,
now,
Resting in his grave....

35. A restart I would like

• 52 •

I would like a restart,
not for you, not for someone,
but for me,
for what I could have been
I once would like a restart,
to spark a fire that's annihilated,
to melt a river that's frozen,
for a burnt star to be reborn,
to win a race that's lost,
to be the great, that I couldn't,
I would like a restart
I don't know what happened,
how the present darkened,
was it,
for pride, for love, for greed,
for bad or for the good,
whatever it was,
it has it roots dwelled deep,
and,
I would like them uprooted,
for once,
I would like a restart.....

36. Distance from the world

I love my distance,
from the world above,
and the people beyond,
but, I get the visit,
from the ones I wittingly resist,
the Moon and the Sun...
The moon,
pierces the fog and mist,
making surrenders to it's gist,
spreading it's light,
with eyes as bright,
and it starts,
a threat to the heart...
And then comes the Sun,
for me ,the world to get,
it brings me my sunset,
to play it part,
a dagger through the heart..
I love my distance,
as I close the gate,
with theb moon's beauty to take,
Knowing,
beautiful sunset will always be my fate.....

37. A good change

I don't care ,
is what,
I have always said,
and believed,
but that's surely changed,
I changed, l.....
I changed,
the moment you waved,
I changed, in ways,
I thought I couldn't change,
change has always scared me,
often scarred me,
but you,
you made me belieleive,
change is good,
and I changed for good,
you changed,
the chaos inside me,
to harmony,
the possibilities to opportunities,
all my negativity to positivity,
and my thoughts to actions,
you changed me,
changed me for good......

38. A shattered heart

You don't know,

How it shatters my heart,

Nobody does,

you are gone,

Maybe forever,

But when I saw you,

Sitting on that bench,

It bothered me,

It's shouldn't,

and It's not right,

but it did,

and I can't help it, but wonder,

What have I done wrong,

To be a bystander as you pass ,

To be the silent member of your class,

To be in that silent empty chamber,

where there's no one to talk to,

no one to hold, the shattered pieces,

to collect the, cremated ashes.....

nobody knows,

except,

the diary that I hold,

the pen,

when I go bold,

and write, about the night,

when I spoke,

and my pillow cried,

unless my eyes dried,
I spoke......

39. A failure

Sometimes......
Waiting in that period ,
Of hope,
of terror,
of fright,
Thinking about the choices made,
About the action delayed
He just prayed, in the period
Of numerous possibility, of
unprecedented inevitability
Waiting.......
Sometimes......
Walking down the road,
With his head lost and shoulders down,
Thinking about the crossroad,
Drown in his thought
What had fate brought him
All the wonders passing on a whim,
Somewhere....
Walking up the staircase
Taking up the disappointed case,
All of which went without a trace,
His mind went numb,
The moment was disheartening,
He had everything but nothing,
Once again,
Standing on the square one,

He was there again alone.........

40. September

These roads I wander,
felt like a familiar stranger,
the dream of heaven,
in these alpine roads,
in a month to remember You,
my September......

A path to you,
is yet to be found,
in the trail of slopes,
a Path to aroma of rain,
a morning on the snowy peak,
nights of starlight,
a path to my forever,
to you, my September.......
With wilderness in my veins,
and Chaos in my heart,
I don't care about reality,
or the escape,
as of my dreams,
Miss September you are mine.....

41. It's you

it's all over the place, yet invisible,
it's obvious, yet unpredicted,
it's the truth, yet uncovered,
it's a bliss, yet to ber found,
it's love, yet to be loved,
it shouldn't be you, yet it's you

42. My burning ship

A burning ship,
On the shore of heartbreak,
In the flames of ,
Doubt and ignorance,
I protect hope's flower,
Whose bloom,
Is worth the everything....
But
Why does it bother me?
It's just a flower,
Of my mere imagination,
Maybe a enchanted flower,
But just a flower,
it means the world to me,
So what,
It's just a flower,
Of my mere imagination......
It was never my trait,
To be the knight,
To be a hero,
Who holds the flower,
But yes,
I always wanted,
To be the one,
Who holds,
The enchanted flower....

But now,

My ship's burning,

On the shore of heartbreak.....

43. The unwritten poem

Hope, the poems touched your heart as they were meant to do